SPACE

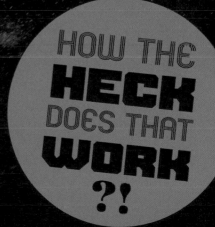

HOW THE **HECK** DOES THAT **WORK** ?!

VIRGINIA LOH-HAGAN

45TH PARALLEL PRESS

Published in the United States of America by Cherry Lake Publishing Group
Ann Arbor, Michigan
www.cherrylakepublishing.com

Reading Adviser: Beth Walker Gambro, MS, Ed., Reading Consultant, Yorkville, IL
Book Designer: Felicia Macheske

Photo Credits: © Delpixel/Shutterstock, cover, 1; © Nikolaeva, cover, back cover, 1; © sripfoto/Shutterstock, cover, back cover, 1; © Yes058 Montree Nanta/Shutterstock, back cover, 10, 11; © Pike-28/Shutterstock, back cover; © John A Davis/Shutterstock, 4; © MicroOne/Shutterstock, 5; © NASA/JPL-Caltech/MSSS, 6; © NASA, 1, 7, 28, 30; © Valerio Pardi/Shutterstock, 8; © Ferenc Speder/Shutterstock, 10; © Science History Images / Alamy Stock Photo, 12; © Yurii Andreichyn/Shutterstock, 14; © Artur Balytskyi/Shutterstock, 13,17; © Agencia Estado/ AP Photo, 15; © Zack Frank/Shutterstock, 16; © Serguei Levykin/Shutterstock, 18; © DGIM studio/Shutterstock, 19; © VectorPot/Shutterstock, 19; © Buntoon Rodseng/Shutterstock, 19; © Bruce Rolff/Shutterstock, 20; © Drawlab19/Shutterstock, 22; © Dotted Yeti/Shutterstock, 23; © sdecoret/Shutterstock, 24; © Fine Art Studio/ Shutterstock, 26; © CkyBe/Shutterstock, 26; © muratart/Shutterstock, 27; © Pete Pahham/Shutterstock, 31

45th Parallel Press is an imprint of Cherry Lake Publishing Group.

Library of Congress Cataloging-in-Publication Data

Names: Loh-Hagan, Virginia, author.
Title: Weird science : space / by Virginia Loh-Hagan.
Description: Ann Arbor, Michigan : Cherry Lake Publishing, [2021]
   | Series: How the heck does that work?! | Includes bibliographical references and
   index.
Identifiers: LCCN 2021004930 (print) | LCCN 2021004931 (ebook)
   | ISBN 9781534187610 (hardcover) | ISBN 9781534189010 (paperback)
   | ISBN 9781534190412 (pdf) | ISBN 9781534191815 (ebook)
Subjects: LCSH: Astronomy—Juvenile literature. | Outer space—Juvenile
   literature.
Classification: LCC QB46 .L834 2021 (print) | LCC QB46 (ebook) | DDC
   523—dc23
LC record available at https://lccn.loc.gov/2021004930
LC ebook record available at https://lccn.loc.gov/2021004931

Cherry Lake Publishing Group would like to acknowledge the work of the Partnership for 21st Century Learning, a Network of Battelle for Kids. Please visit *http://www.battelleforkids.org/networks/p21* for more information.

Printed in the United States of America
Corporate Graphics

Dr. Virginia Loh-Hagan is an author, university professor, and former classroom teacher. She's currently the Director of the Asian Pacific Islander Desi American Resource Center at San Diego State University. She loves science-fiction stories. She lives in San Diego with her very tall husband and very naughty dogs.

TABLE OF CONTENTS

INTRODUCTION.. 5

CHAPTER 1
METEOR SHOWERS.. 9

CHAPTER 2
SPACE JUNK..13

CHAPTER 3
MYSTERIOUS RADIO SIGNAL..........................17

CHAPTER 4
ROGUE PLANETS..21

CHAPTER 5
BLACK HOLES...25

CHAPTER 6
BLACK SPACE...29

GLOSSARY...32

LEARN MORE...32

INDEX...32

Earth is in the Milky Way galaxy.

INTRODUCTION

All kinds of weird science happen in space. Outer space is the empty areas that house the **universe**. The universe is huge. It's everything that exists. This includes planets and stars. It includes everything on Earth.

The universe contains billions of **galaxies**. Galaxies are huge space collections. They're made up of billions of stars, gas, and dust. They include **solar** systems. Solar means having to do with the sun. These galaxies spin very fast in space. There's a lot of space between stars and galaxies. This space is filled with dust, light, heat, and rays. This space is called the intergalactic medium (IGM).

Scientists study space. They create tools to study space. They make rockets. They send people to space. **Astronauts** are people trained to fly to space. They explore space.

Scientists study the things in space. They want to see if life is possible on other planets. They want to see if there are other life forms. We know a lot about space. But there's so much we don't know. We want to learn more.

Dare to learn more about space science! So much is going on. How the heck does it all work?

NASA stands for National Aeronautics and Space Administration. It's the U.S. space program.

Space objects include comets and asteroids.

CHAPTER 1

METEOR SHOWERS

When was the last time you looked up into the sky? Earth circles the Sun. It goes through patches of dust clouds. These clouds have space rocks. Some of these rocks enter Earth's **atmosphere**. Atmosphere is the layer of gases surrounding planets. When these space rocks enter Earth's atmosphere, they're called **meteors**.

A meteor falls toward Earth. It drags as it falls. This happens because the air in the atmosphere pushes against the meteor. This drag is very hot. It burns brightly as it passes through the atmosphere. It looks like a bright streak. The bright streak is not the rock. It's the glowing hot air.

Meteor showers are named for the constellation from which they appear to come. Constellations are groups of stars.

Sometimes, lots of meteors fall to Earth. They do this in a short period of time. Their tails point back to the same spot in the sky. They're coming to us from the same angle. This is called a meteor shower.

Some meteors are big rocks. But most are small. They're often smaller than a grain of sand. They quickly burn up in the atmosphere. This means they won't hit Earth's surface. There's no harm to humans.

Sometimes, meteors survive through Earth's atmosphere. They explode high in the air. Bits may fall to Earth. They're known as meteorites.

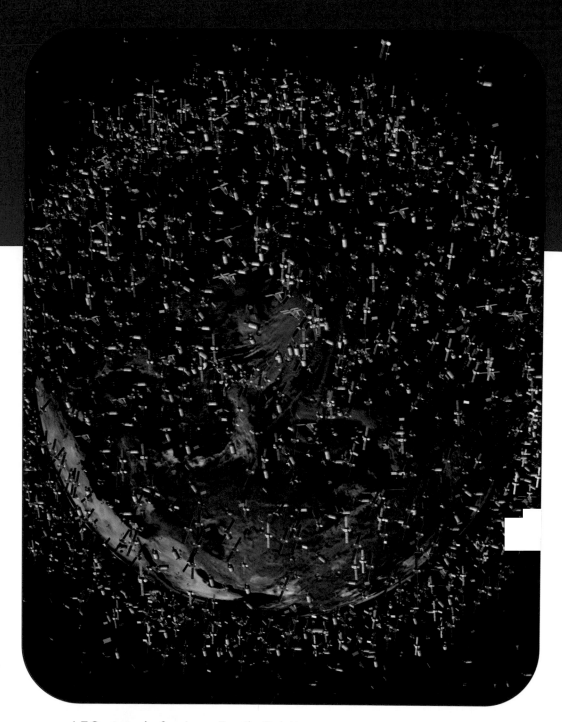

LEO stands for Low Earth Orbit.
LEO is an orbital space junkyard.

CHAPTER 2

SPACE JUNK

What do you do with your trash? You throw it away. But what about space? There's trash in space. Space trash could be broken bits from space objects. Trash in space could also come from human-made objects or trash. Human trash includes broken **spacecraft**. Spacecraft are vehicles used to travel in space. Space trash includes spacecraft parts. It includes paint chips from rockets.

More than 100 million pieces of space junk circle Earth. They travel up to 17,500 miles (28,164 kilometers) per hour. They could crash into spacecraft. Space junk could also push spacecraft off their **orbits**. Orbits are paths. More space junk means more dangers to spacecraft.

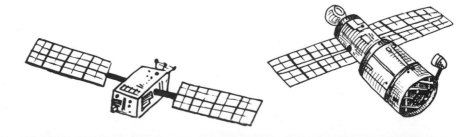

Even WEIRDER SPACE SCIENCE!

- Jupiter and Saturn are gas planets. Lightning storms turn methane gas into soot. The soot has lots of carbon. As soot falls, it hardens into graphite chunks. The chunks turn into diamonds. These diamond hailstones melt into a liquid sea.

- The Moon landing left boot prints on the Moon. These boot prints will be there for millions of years. This is because the Moon has no atmosphere. There's no water to wipe away the prints. There's no wind. Wind pushes things around. It spreads things around in the air. Without wind and water, nothing moves.

- Exoplanets are planets outside of our solar system. Gliese 436 b is an exoplanet. It's about 30 light years away from Earth. A light year refers to space distance. It's the distance light travels in 1 year. It's a superlong distance! Exoplanets have different water elements. The ice on the planet stays solid due to pressure despite the planet's hot temperature. The pressure from gravity forms burning ice! Gravity is a force that causes things to fall toward Earth's center.

Scientists track space junk that's larger than a softball. They inspect spacecraft when they return to Earth. They check to see what's missing.

They also use special tools such as **lasers**. Lasers measure the distance of objects. Laser beams hit the junk in orbit. They bounce back to Earth. Scientists measure how long it takes to figure out where they are and where they're going. These lasers only work for a few hours at twilight. This is when Earth is dark. The space junk shines in the sky. It's lit up by the Sun.

Scientists are making new tools to track in daylight.

There aren't any international space laws to clean up space junk.

Astronomers use different types
of telescopes to study space.

CHAPTER 3

MYSTERIOUS RADIO SIGNAL

Have you ever heard strange noises? Scientists scan for radio signals. In 2019, they heard a mysterious radio signal. The signal came from Proxima Centauri. This is the closest galaxy to us. It's about 4.2 light years away.

Proxima Centauri is a solar system. It has 2 planets. One planet may be like Earth. That's where scientists picked up a signal. They heard narrow beams of radio waves. They named the signal BLC1. BLC1 means Breakthrough Listen Candidate 1.

BLC1 passed through all of the filters. Scientists used the Parkes radio telescope. This telescope isdesigned to receive radio waves from space.

The Parkes radio telescope has a **dish antenna**. The dish collects incoming radio waves. It's more than 200 feet (61 meters) wide. Due to its size, it can collect faint sounds.

The Parkes radio telescope has a **receiver**. The receiver boosts weak radio signals. It amplifies the signal about a million times.

The Parkes radio telescope has a **recorder**. This records the signal. Signals are saved on computers.

Parkes radio telescope is in Australia. It's one of the largest dishes in the southern part of the world.

UNSOLVED MYSTERY

Many movies and books are about aliens. But are they real? Humans have been searching for extraterrestrial life for years. Extraterrestrial means being from outside Earth. Extraterrestrial life could be space aliens. It could be microbes. Microbes are tiny organisms. Earth microbes can survive in extreme places. This makes people believe in extraterrestrial life. Some people believe aliens have made contact with us. Crop circles are strange patterns made in farm fields. They mysteriously appear overnight. Some people think aliens made them. Some people think they've seen aliens. Some think aliens kidnap people. Some think they've seen alien spaceships. But scientists say there's no proof of aliens. That doesn't stop people from looking or believing. It doesn't stop people from telling stories about aliens.

Without suns, rogue planets are cold and dark.

CHAPTER 4

ROGUE PLANETS

Did you know some planets are **orphans**? Orphan means not having parents. Orphan planets are also called **rogue** planets. Rogue means being out of order. Rogue planets do their own thing. They don't orbit a sun directly. They're free from their "parent" suns.

Scientists believe there are more than 50 billion rogue planets in the Milky Way. They're wandering in outer space. They move without orbiting. Some rogue planets are 3 times bigger than Earth. They're hard to find. They don't give off any light. Without a sun, they have no light to reflect. Scientists are still learning about rogue planets.

TEST IT OUT!

The universe hasn't always been the same size. It also hasn't always existed. Some scientists believe it began with a "Big Bang." This is a theory. A theory is an idea based on facts. The Big Bang theory explains how the universe was born. First, the universe was 1 hot, thick blob. Then, a big blast blew it up. This happened 10 to 20 billion years ago. Next, energy spread out. Last, stars and planets formed. This all happened in less than a second. Scientists think the universe is still expanding. Expanding means growing or spreading out. Learn more about how the universe expands.

Materials

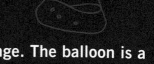

- Balloon
- Clip
- Black marker

1. Blow up a balloon. Make it the size of an orange. The balloon is a model of the universe.

2. Clip the balloon closed.

3. Draw dots on the balloon with a black marker. The dots represent planets.

4. Remove the clip. Keep blowing up the balloon. Watch what happens to the dots. This shows how the universe is expanding.

The process of forming planets is messy. Space objects bang into one another. Bits can join and form planets. But sometimes, the bangs are too violent. They kick out planets. This is what causes rogue planets.

Rogue planets can also form without a bang. Some are failed stars. There's a cloud of gas and dust. Instead of forming into a star, this cloud breaks down. It becomes a rogue planet.

In some cases, solar systems may travel too close to each other. Their orbits mix. They disturb each other. Orbits could fling out rogue planets.

Some rogue planets have moons.

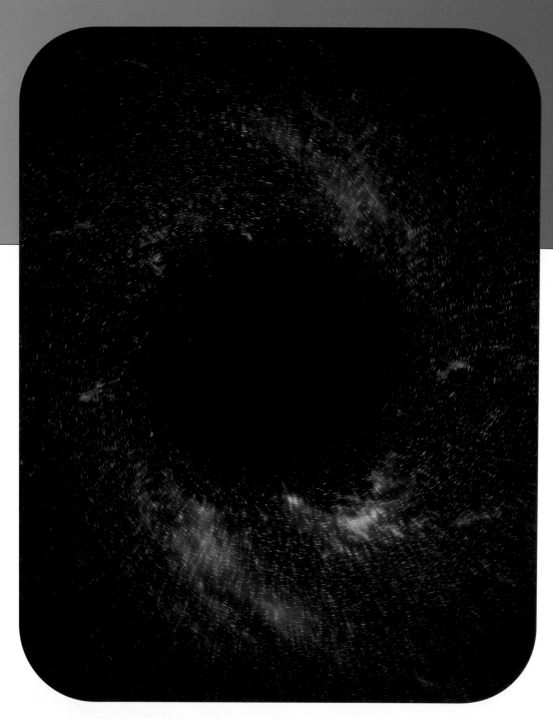

Scientists have no idea what's happening in black holes.

CHAPTER 5

BLACK HOLES

Have you heard about black holes? Black holes are **dense** areas in space. Dense means crowded and solid. Black holes make deep gravity sinks. The deeper the gravity sinks, the more space distorts and curves.

Black holes have strong gravity. They have a strong pull. They don't suck things in. They force things to fall into them. They pull so much that nothing escapes. Light can't even escape. This means black holes can't be seen. It's why they're black.

The boundary of black holes is called the "**event horizon**." This is the point of no return. Matter, like light, can get in. But it can't get out. It doesn't travel anywhere. It "disappears."

SCIENTIST SPOTLIGHT

Alyssa Carson is an astronaut-in-training. She's the youngest to graduate from the Advanced Space Academy program at 16 years old. She's from Louisiana. At age 3, she watched a show about space travel. This sparked her passion about space. Since then, she's dreamed of going to Mars. At age 5, she went to her first space camp. She's attended more than 19 space camps. In 2014, Carson was the first person to complete the "NASA Passport Program." This means she visited all of NASA's 14 visitor centers across 9 states. At age 18, she earned her pilot's license. She is studying astrobiology at the Florida Institute of Technology. She writes about space. She gives speeches and has appeared on TV shows. She promotes space-themed products. Carson said, "We need to get more women working across all of those fields, in all sorts of STEM careers." STEM stands for science, technology, engineering, and math.

Black holes fling out spitballs. These spitballs are made of gas, dust, and matter. This material comes from **accretion disks** before passing into event horizons. Accretion disks are rings around black holes. They orbit black holes. They make a lot of energy.

Gravity is strongest at a black hole's center. It **warps** space and time. Warp means to twist or bend. The center is known as **singularity**. Singularity is a place of **infinitely** dense matter. Infinite means having no limits. This singularity slows down time. As people move closer to the singularity, they'll be pulled in. Time will slow down even more.

Black holes grow in size by taking in galaxy matter. Black holes pull in things. They consume materials that orbit close to them.

The night sky is also dark. Stars are
too far away to shine light.

CHAPTER 6

BLACK SPACE

Do you know why space is black? Many scientists have thought about this. They've studied pictures and sounds. They came up with theories. Heinrich Wilhelm Olbers was a German scientist. He was one of the first to come up with a theory. Olbers questioned the universe being infinite. He believed the universe would one day die. It's not stable. Galaxies are expanding. They're speeding away in different directions. We can't see stars everywhere. This is because there is a limited number of stars. Also, many stars are too young. Their light isn't strong enough to reach us. That's why we see black.

There are different types of radiation in space.

Some scientists focus on light waves. The color black means there's no light. But the solar system is filled with light. There are many stars. These stars are really far apart. Light moves in a straight line. It reflects off something. Or it's bent by a lens. However,, most of outer space is empty. Light is taken in by this space. This means we only see black.

Light from other galaxies struggles to reach Earth. It comes to us as **radiation**. Radiation refers to energy waves. As the universe expands, light waves are stretched out. They become radiation waves. We can't see these waves. That's why space seems black to us. Scientists are still discovering new things about space.

GLOSSARY

accretion disks (uh-KREE-shuhn DISKS) rings or haloes around black holes

astronauts (ASS-truh-nawts) people trained to explore and study space

atmosphere (AT-muhss-fihr) layer of gases surrounding planets

dense (DENSS) crowded and compacted, solid

dish antenna (DISH an-TEN-uh) tool shaped like a dish that collects incoming radio waves

event horizon (i-vent huh-RYE-zuhn) boundary of black holes where matter can get in but not out

galaxies (GAL-uhk-seez) huge space collections made of billions of stars, gas, and dust

infinitely (IN-fuh-nit-lee) without an end or limits

lasers (LAY-zurs) very powerful beams of light

meteors (MEE-tee-urs) space rocks that enter Earth's atmosphere

orbits (OR-bitz) paths that circle around

orphans (OR-fuhns) children without parents

radiation (ray-dee-AY-shuhn) energy waves

receiver (ri-SEE-vur) tool that takes in and amplifies signals

recorder (ri-KOR-dur) tool that saves signals for future reference

rogue (ROHG) being out of order

singularity (sin-gyoo-LAIR-uh-tee) the center of a black hole

solar (SOH-lur) having to do with the sun

spacecraft (SPAYSS-kraft) vehicles that travel in space

universe (YOO-nuh-vurss) everything that exists, including planets, stars, and space

warps (WORPZ) distorts, twists, or bends

LEARN MORE

Loh-Hagan, Virginia. *Black Holes*. Ann Arbor, MI: Cherry Lake Publishing, 2021.

Loh-Hagan, Virginia. *Lost in Space Hacks*. Ann Arbor, MI: Cherry Lake Publishing, 2019.

Morgan, Ben, ed. *Space! The Universe As You've Never Seen It Before*. New York, NY: DK Publishing, 2015.

Tyson, Neil deGrasse. *StarTalk: Young Readers Edition*. Washington, DC: National Geographic Kids, 2018.

INDEX

accretion disks, 27
aliens, 19
antenna, dish, 18
asteroids, 8
astronauts, 6, 26
astronomers, 16
atmosphere, 9, 11, 14

Big Bang theory, 22
black holes, 24–27
black space, 28–31

carbon, 14
Carson, Alyssa, 26
comets, 8
constellations, 10
crop circles, 19

diamonds, 14
dish antenna, 18
dust, 9, 27
Earth, 4, 11, 25
energy, 27, 31
event horizon, 25, 27
exoplanets, 14
extraterrestrial life, 19

galaxies, 4, 5, 17, 29, 31
gas planets, 14
gases, 5, 9, 27
gravity, 25, 27

infinity, 27, 29

Jupiter, 14

lasers, 15
LEO (Low Earth Orbit), 12
light, 16, 17, 21, 25, 28, 29, 31
light year, 17

matter, 25, 27
meteor showers, 8–11
meteorites, 11
microbes, 19
moon, 14, 23

NASA (National Aeronautics and Space Administration), 7

Olbers, Heinrich Wilhelm, 29
orbits, 13, 23
orphan planets, 21

Parkes radio telescope, 18
planets, 14, 17, 22
    formation process, 23
    rogue, 20–23
Proxima Centauri, 17

radiation, 30, 31
radio signals, mysterious, 16–18
radio telescopes, 16, 18
rogue planets, 20–23

Saturn, 14
singularity, 27
solar systems, 5, 14, 17, 23, 31
space
    introduction, 4–7
    mystery, 19
    weird science, 14

s (*continued*)
space junk, 12–15
spacecraft, 13, 15
spitballs, 27
stars, 5, 10, 22, 23, 28, 29, 31
suns, 20, 21

telescopes, 16, 18
time, 27
trash, 13

universe, 5, 22, 24, 29